Live Laugh Love

Like a Teenager

Karina Williams

ARCHWAY
PUBLISHING

Archway Publishing books may be ordered through booksellers or by contacting:

Archway Publishing
1663 Liberty Drive
Bloomington, IN 47403
www.archwaypublishing.com
1 (888) 242-5904

ISBN: 978-1-4808-3224-4 (sc)
ISBN: 978-1-4808-3225-1 (e)

Library of Congress Control Number: 2016908717

Print information available on the last page.

Archway Publishing rev. date: 6/30/2016

This book is dedicated to my lovely family, my wonderful friends, my cover artist Olivia Magon, and my outstanding English teachers Mrs. Hillesland and Ms. Mann. This is also for all those beautiful souls who know what it means to live.

Contents

Unspoken

Behind those smiles are too many tears,
    Tears that have been hiding for too many years,
        Years that have been bad in too many ways,
            Ways that keep changing for too many days,
                Days that drag on for far too long,
                Too long to hold back things too wrong,
            Wrong feelings, wrong people, far too much,
        Too much to hold back, too far to touch
      Those unreachable things; too many broken,
Broken all because of those words, too many
Unspoken.

My Rap

It's really just not worth it, all of this pain.
Because of you, for me there is no gain.
I'm leaving you, but you might see me around.
Don't come looking; I don't want to be found.
Yeah, I'm here, just not around you.
'Cause you only ever give me one thing to do:
Listen to you whine, "She doesn't even care."
Or maybe even, "This is so unfair."
I listened to your problems, helped you out.
But I'm done, and it's really just about
Time I am leaving, or I'll miss my reservation
To a place called my life; I'm taking my vacation.

A Different Story

These feelings I have, I just don't know
    how to put them into words in a way that will show
        you how I feel, not a piece left out.
            So let me try to tell you what this is all about.
You see, we became friends a long time ago.
    I wasn't sure it would be so, but I went with the flow.
        We became friends; then even later
            we found something real,
                something even greater
than anything known to us. I had no clue
    that one day I would learn to depend on you.
        But it fell apart, broken and s h a t t e r e d.
            We couldn't find the pieces, all of them scattered.
                The friendship was gone, everything dismissed.
I had to hold back telling you about how much I missed
    the way we used to be, just us two.
        We were better than best friends, something new,
            something we created out of all we had been through.
But maybe, just maybe, if you had missed me too…
    We could be great again, but different; we'd do more than shine.
        This time we'd be perfect, and you would be
all mine.

A Child

A child's laugh, young and innocent,
high, ringing, and full of youth,
asks questions about the unknown world.
Without getting answers, there lies only a secret
behind that heart-shaped smile.

Preteen eyes saying, "Catch me if you can,"
running from the past, chasing the future,
ready to take on time and challenge it to run out,
not knowing that life waits for no one
until it's over.

Was It Worth It?

With the good things we get, there is a price to pay.
That doesn't mean we can't have a say
in what it does to us, the choices we make.
Does it make us happy?
Does it make us feel sad?
Is this thing really good, or could it be really bad?
The question still stands:
... Is it worth it?

Can anything be regretted, even a little bit?
Because if the answer is no, then give it your all.
Walk slowly to the edge and just take a step
into this chance, take a risk, dare to fall.
Because sooner or later, it will all be done
... if it is worth it.

Then you will see the greatness of what has begun.
No regrets because you dared to step out
when you were young and had to choose
to take a chance and dared to lose.
Because now we are older and wiser, too.
We can answer the question that I asked:
... Was it worth it?
And after that, it would be that time again when
we see our kids, asking the same question
with hope
and innocence
and love.
They really just want to know
if this choice is okay, if it's right,
... if it was truly worth it.

Lock and Key

The sparks between them, they are so real.
It's like nothing he thought he would ever feel.
Already these sparks have set his heart on fire;
saying he doesn't love her would make him a liar.
For him, there is no way to live without her.
She makes him wish he could stay forever,
right here, right now, but they need to wait.
If they end up together, it must be fate.
He knows they love each other; nothing will break them apart.
She has and always will have the key to his heart.

Too Much

It hurts to see her like this. He doesn't know
how she can do this to herself— how can she show
anything she is not? She tries to hide everything.
She keeps saying to forget the lingering
feeling of anger and disappointment inside of him.
Though he just wants her honesty, to go out on a limb,
he is concerned; he doesn't understand why.
He wants her to stop holding it all inside.
"Talk to me," he says, "and we'll get by."
He's angry, so angry at her, but maybe at himself too.
'Cause she cannot see everything she is
to everyone. They all care so much, too considerably,
to see her do this to herself, to ignore the hurt
she gives to herself; if only she knew
that he wants her and he needs her to be all right.
Because in the end, she is not alone in this fight.

Start Over

I was really counting on you. I needed you.
But of course you let me down; you always do.
Tired of canceled plans or just plain being rejected.
I am done with this, tired of being dejected.
This is over—we're over—I think it's time for me
to find new friends, a new life. I need to be free.
So leave, get out; I need time to think.
I need to find something, maybe the next link
of my life, so I can start over and really try
to forget about us; so let's start now
with goodbye.

Sooner or Later

Sooner or later
I swear
I'm going to lose
Myself
Just like
I lose
Everyone
Else.

Sometimes

Sometimes
when it's dark outside
and the world around goes silent,
the mind,
it wanders, so loud,
louder than silence could ever be.
And it makes you wonder,
How big am I to this world?

Sometimes
when the sun is shining
and the world around gets brighter,
all the people,
they seem so happy,
happiness that can be found inside.
And it makes you wonder,
How easy is it to be happy?

And sometimes
when the rain is falling
and the world around becomes clean,
all the little pieces,
they come together
to fit perfectly, like the final piece of a puzzle.
And it makes you wonder,
How many lives have found that final piece?

Run

"You break it, you buy it" is not even close.
You break this heart, and you'll never get it back.
And if that happens, you're gonna need a dose
of happiness, 'cause when I'm done, you'd better pack
your bags and flee, and you'd better run fast.
'Cause if I find you—oh, you'd better hope I don't—
my pretty face is gonna be the last
thing you see if you get caught.
Run faster. I'm almost there,
but don't worry—I won't touch your face,
just your dreams, because I'm your nightmare.
Because if you break it, you'll need a saving grace.
Better start running.
Fast.

Love,
Me

One Way or Another

I don't know whether to give up, to let it go, or hold onto us, though I really don't know
what we have left, if you want me talking to you or even trying to be a part of your life.
I guess friends is okay, too, but I really need to know what it is you are feeling.
Are we friends? Are we totally done? Is there a new relationship you have begun?
I don't know about you, but we need to talk because I need to know if you are going to lock me out of your life.
Can we still be friends, or is it too late to make amends between us?
If you do want to try, then we can make something work.
I know I would feel better if we could just be okay
as friends, if nothing more.
I still love you either way.

Just Us Two

The best of times, the worst of times,
together, me and you.
We would be together, me and you.
Best friends always, me and you.
You were always there to pull me through.
Stay together, me and you.
Always?

But soon those words became untrue.
Untrue, me and you.
Something happened; something changed.
A wall was built between us two.
We thought we could make it, me and you,
but that wall, it just grew between me and you.

New friends came, and new friends stayed.
Soon you were out of my view.
We stopped talking, me and you;
the spaces between us grew and grew.
I wanted that back, just us two.
There was so much I missed about us.
I needed you; that much was true.
I needed us to be able to pull through.
But now there is no more
me and you.

Tragedies

Tragedies only seem to be tragic when the world hears about them. But what about those internal fights people have every day, when someone suffers alone? What about what happens behind closed doors, the tragedies we do not see, like a child cutting himself or loud family fights over the dinner table? What about the abusive parents or spouses and those parents who are never sober enough to kiss their children goodnight? What about a month after the tragedy? Will people still care, still be willing to change? What happens then—will we fold or will we fight? And what do we do about the tragedies we don't see—the ones we don't quite understand? If the world doesn't know, is it still a tragedy?

Our Generation

We long for the days we can't remember,
those childhood days with all of our friends.
We had one group; everyone was a member.
The big things were cartwheels and back-bends.
There was no drama; a bad word was "stupid."
Everyone got along. No nerds, no geeks;
nobody cared or even thought about Cupid.
We were all so innocent, silly stickers on our cheeks.
What happened to that? Did we all just grow up?
Found new friends, became popular or not...
The main thing now is a make-up or break-up.
What about our old friends, the ones we forgot?
We want it to be easier, but we're not working together.
Why not go back to our innocence, just start a conversation
by saying "hi," and instantly have a bond like brothers?
What happened to that? What happened to our generation?

People Matter

There's only one person anyone can be.
Only you can be you, and I can be me.
There's only so much one person can achieve,
so remember to give no matter what you receive.
Kindness is the key to anyone's heart,
and it will never be too late to start.
Loved ones need to be cherished and cared for,
because in our lives they are what matters more
than anyone or anything. They have shaped us
into who we are and they are everything that drives us.
So make sure they know where your heart is set,
because when the clocks runs down
there is no reset.

Thoughts

Such restless thoughts, which my mind cannot control,
  Spilling out from beneath my soul
In charcoal like wisps of confusion and guilt
    Intertwined with pastels of certainty and delight
And the blinding pain of it all

Stuck

Looking ahead, the future is where we are all going in five minutes, five years, and five centuries from now. We will fall in love, graduate, break hearts, and live life because what else is there do with all of that time?

So why not be a little crazy, let go of all sanity, be free, take a deep breath, look up and smile? This is supposed to be the time of our lives. We are the only thing holding ourselves back now, with the lies we tell and the amount of times we trip over our own two feet, but we can get back up. We will begin running once again, searching and looking for where we belong and who we really are inside. It is a secret that only time can hold from us, like the truth, locked away where it will never be found.

Try as we might, looking forward now, we will never reach the future—after all, we will always be stuck in the present.

Focus

It's funny how the world seems to fall away
    and everything goes quiet
while all of your energy is focused
    on someone or something you love.
All the problems, the stress
    the goodbyes, the heartbreak—it all
      fades away
until the only thing left that matters
    in the world is
      that person.

Let It Go

I see you so much, there's no avoiding you.
Am I back to the start, still not over us?
Who you are to me has changed so much—
I liked who you were, but now
you are an ordinary boy, but that's just it...
You were *my* boy and this changes us a bit
because those feelings I had will not fade away.
I want to be over you, but they want to stay.
I can't get over it, and I see you too much
to get over what is left, my feelings and such.
I need some space, but where can I go?
I must simply go forward, not too high or too low,
to just let it all go, and finally be free,
to stop worrying and thinking.
To just be me.

A New Year

A new year will soon start,
with these memories in my heart.
I will remember each and every one
of you, no matter what has been done.
A new year means a second chance
for everyone who missed that last dance.
But before this year ends and we move on,
we should get together and remember the marathon
of things we did together with all of our friends,
or maybe end a fight and try to make amends.
Because this new year is coming, and from what I've seen,
it's going to be an amazing 2013.

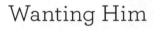

Wanting Him

You know those feelings that you get
When you can't stop thinking about him
And you know that you should stop
As you know it can't be healthy
For a heart to beat so fast
And breathing to become so hard,
That this shouldn't be happening,
Not to you, not this way,
But there can be a small chance
That maybe you don't want to stop
And maybe you want him on your mind,
To see his smile everywhere,
To hear his laugh in every heartbeat,
The possibility of this being
Right where you need to be,
That maybe there's only one reason
For these feelings to get so crazy,
That maybe it's not the feeling you want.
Maybe you just want
Him.

Tell Me...

Tell me to walk away, and I will run to you.
Tell me to never look back, and I will turn around.
Tell me to move on, and I will retrace my steps.
Tell me that the story is over, and I will write another chapter.
Tell me to never come back, and I will wait for you.
Tell me that you lied, and I will forgive you.
Tell me that you're okay, and I will hold you tight.
Tell me that you are sad, and I will give you a reason to smile.
But, tell me that you love me, and I will tell you...

I love you back.

Simplicity

Life itself is simple—simple, yet hard to hold,
hard to understand what it is you're being told.
Sometimes you're told to walk, other times maybe run.
To focus on work, then have a little fun.
Words can be confusing in the simplest of ways,
hard to figure out, in our minds for days,
but once finally understood, everything is clear.
Things are meant to be close, kept very near
to the heart and to the soul, others far away.
All of this from life, all of this to say—
simplicity is complicated, sometimes smaller than a dimple,
but dimples equal smiles, and smiles are quite simple.
So smile when you can, and make life kinda easy
to melt all the complications into a quiet simplicity.

Set Free

I'm tired of not being able to be seen,
on the outside of jokes, not knowing what they mean.
Posting pictures everywhere of all your friends—
I just want to know when will it end?
Anywhere I turn, any place I go,
you're posing in pictures just to make a show.
Do you just not see me? Do you even care?
All I feel like is a shadow in the air.
What can I do? Which way can I turn?
I feel like just another picture to burn.
Why can't you see what you've done to me?
I need to be found; I need to be set free.

My Eyes

Your eyes are blue, beautiful, wild, and free
as I stare into them and everything is lost on me.
My eyes are brown, but I never knew what they meant,
how much you loved them, or why you spent
so much time and love staring into them.
You would think they were some kind of priceless gem.
No, they are just eyes, but I now know why
you love them so much. They help identify
who I am, the girl you love with the big brown eyes.
And you, the boy with the blue eyes, you have made me realize
that my eyes are just a part of me, showing me who I will be.
The girl who loves the blue-eyed boy; that I guarantee.

Definition of Love

Look into my eyes and tell me what you see:
    a bit of a smile hiding someone who is lonely,
      maybe a hint of mischief and a wild side,
        an uneven boundary where crazy and sane collide.
Listen to my heart and tell me what you hear.
    Can you hear it beating, loud and clear?
      Dancing to the rhythm, the steady sounds of time,
        slowly ticking away, pounding with every rhyme?
Open up my mind and tell me what you learn,
    the millions of questions you find at every turn,
      with answers that are hidden only to be found
        by someone who knows how to find their way around.
Kiss me on my lips and tell me how you feel:
    is this really worth it? Is this truly real?
      Here is our chance to jump, to try, and if we do,
        then you know that I mean it when I say
          I'm in love with you.

Jump, Then Fall

I've never felt this way before, the way that I do now.
It's completely confusing in so many ways, how
my life gets all chaotic, but I know that it's okay when
I look into your eyes and they sparkle,
asking "Where have ya been?"
Something about that smile perched up on your face,
or that adorable laugh you have when my hair's all out of place—
you make me feel crazy, but amazing, all of the above.
I don't know what to call this; some people call it love.
One way or another, I don't know what to do,
'cause I can't go an hour without thinking about you.
I guess there's only one way to go if we want to hold onto it all,
so let's go with gravity; take my hand and jump, then fall.

I Am From

I am from the quiet, a lover and a dreamer.
Lost in memories of Saturday cartoons and Scooby Doo,
little birthday parties with poppers and streamers,
playing dress-up with my friends and trying on my mother's shoes.

I am from musical instruments and learning how to play
the violin and the piano, all in rhythm together.
Making breakfast as a family every Sunday,
and enjoying the outdoors, no matter what the weather.

I am from a beautiful family, raised with respect:
my mom taught us to be honest and always to be nice.
My dad said to be helpful and always protect
one another because siblings are worth the sacrifice.

I am from cinnamon bun Saturdays and games of cards,
using all the pillows to make forts in the living room.
Late nights roasting marshmallows and
ghost stories of graveyards,
not to forget Halloween, complete with candy and a costume.

I am from holidays spent together with stockings weeks before,
and always opening a present early on Christmas Eve.
Late talks with my brothers and adventures to explore
The world and everything around. I would never believe...

That I am going to college only three years from now,
and I'm aspiring to be a vet, with a writer's and musician's heart.
I hope to change the world. That is my dream somehow,
but I will always be true myself, the quiet dreamer from the start.

You

If only you could see yourself through
my eyes, then you could understand that you
are amazing, sweet, and wonderful in ways
that you need to see through all that haze.
Not to mention how handsome you really are.
If you saw that, your potential could reach so far
beyond what you expect you could be.
You will find Your Girl once she can see
and know that she has found
The One, The Guy that she has been bound
to find and love and start a new
life with, the one, the only you.

Think About It

Maturity is but a state of mind. You know where you are, where you need to go, what you need to do, and the limits you can push to get there.

Never regret a thing you've done, never want to change a thing, because it has already changed everything.

So love where you are, who you are, what you have, and what you don't. Life itself is easy; it is the things you do or don't have that make it hard.

Love is but a word; it is the feeling behind that word that means everything.

We all want to know what is going to happen with our lives, but don't spoil the ending to this story because it has barely even started.

People forget things, things that you might remember as big, but to them, meant nothing. Things happen, and people change. Though life goes on, it still hurts.

We all still have time. I guess it's just part of growing up—make friends, lose friends, cry, be happy, get our feelings hurt, remember the little things, forget others ... It's all part of life.

"Summer love doesn't mean turning off your brain. It means opening up your heart."

Getting lost is a part of life. The story only comes when you decide to try to find yourself again.

"Now it's like we're a broken mirror, a broken heart with the pieces scattered. A lock with the key thrown into the bottom of the ocean."

"I feel that a truly great love can only be found by those conscious of time and what it means. Those aware of time do not waste it on fights or platitudes, but rather truth and well-spent moments to make up for the time when we may all be gone."

Close

I ran my hands down your stomach,
the smooth curves of your back.
How could a body be so beautiful
but hidden, only seen to those
who want to know how it feels
beneath skin-deep?

To be so attached, to want someone
so badly it gets harder and harder to breathe,
and finally once you have them ...

Everything finally fits together,
your hands in my hair, my hands
on your neck, your face, your back.
I just want your body beneath my own,
to feel you and know you...
to understand you

and everything may be all right again.
The two of us are beautiful together,
and our bodies just move together
so perfectly, so fluidly, like it was
meant to be.

Best Friend

Best friends forever, that's what they say.
They have your back each and every day.
Those inside jokes no one else will know,
the simple little smile that will always show
that they know what you think without a single word.
A whole conversation of looks, though no one heard,
you make a sound because you can just tell
what they would have said—you know them that well.
Best friends are best friends; they have their way
of lasting, like love when it wants to stay.
So just go with the flow and enjoy those moments
of uncontrollable laughter, live life to its extent.
Because that's all you can do, knowing that when
it's all over, you will never be that young again, ever.

Childhood

We were born and raised in a beautiful place.
We learned and grew at a steady pace,
taught to love as we loved to learn
that we only deserve the things we earn.
As we grew older, we got wiser;
things made more sense, no need for an advisor.
Then even later, we could look back:
"Those were the days; we used to do track."
There were things that we did and people we met;
sometimes we got a little upset.
Childhood memories, oh, they were good,
but redoing anything... I never would.

Catch Me

Every time you touch me, my skin burns with delight.
This is something that I wish I didn't have to fight.
I shouldn't do this, I can't do this—but I really want to,
for I know you only too well. You're the type of person who
keeps me wanting more of you with me for the rest of my life.
If I miss you for a day, it cuts me like a knife...
Seeing you the next day, it's as if I've been gone for a year.
It's like a deaf person realizing they can hear.
I am falling in your love, falling so deeply. And you,
you just need to catch me.

Falling

I wish I could fall and never have to think
That you would catch me, hoping in just one blink
That everything would be okay and nothing would fall apart,
Nothing crazy would happen and break my heart.
I guess I should trust you … I really need to.
This just feels so right because it's the easiest thing to do.
It's crazy that I like you so much;
I can't figure it out, my feelings and such.
I'm so confused. This has never happened before.
I don't really know, maybe not for sure.
But this has to be like, maybe love too,
and right now, I'm falling really hard for you.

First Kiss

Why do I have to ask myself if I love you?
If I truly did, the answer would be "I do."
Thoughts of you are taking away my reality
but I don't want them to. You said you loved me
and I didn't say it back—there's a reason for that.
You deserve someone who loves you too,
someone who truly cares.
But I just want to chat
with you for hours without a single spat.
That is all I can give you because
I'm not that girl you're looking for.
I'm sorry for this.
Someone else is going to be yours and worth the
first kiss.

A Broken Heart

Alone again on Valentine's Day,
all because I didn't know what to say.
I was so nervous when you came to me.
The thought never crossed my mind that we
would end up together. So when I caught
you looking at me and finally got
the feeling of love that we shared.
You showed me that you really cared.
Until I broke your heart,
for I had not a clue...
But you should know
that my heart
has broken too.

Ten Million to One

Sitting here in a quiet place, all I can think about
is how badly I want to scream, how I really want to shout
that all I really need is someone to show me love.
Someone who can prosper and excel so far above
what I really want so that I can say "I love you,"
and maybe even later end up saying "I do."
First I need it to start with one little glance,
or maybe a single hello while we dance.
Sparks might fly and then we can get to know
each other. Soon after we will begin to show
our feelings, and what our love can really be:
many moments of laughter, happiness, and glee.
You can be my best friend, everything under the sun.
Let's beat the odds of us finding each other, ten million to one.

The Truth

Things we don't say, the things we hold back—
sometimes we regret it, our minds keeping track
of every single one, if we could just have said it.
Told people what we think and not a little bit
of hurt come from it, all feelings the same.
We should not have to play this game
because it's just the truth—nothing less, nothing more.
This shouldn't be played with or turned into a chore.
We just want people to know what we believe,
where no one reacts, no person deceived.
Just to get it out there, to say how we feel,
to know what's really happening, that this is all real.
Have you ever held back, though something needed to be said?
Well, this one's for you, to say it next time instead.

Perpetuity

In that moment when you opened your eyes,
the day you were born,
you gained two lives:
the life that is yours—you only get one—
everything you are
and everything you may become.
Then there is that second life, almost for free,
joining with the lives of others,
becoming one with immortality.
That second life you have, it will always be here
in the memories, caught in pictures
of those you love, whom you hold dear.
And in that tragic moment when the first one is lost,
touching every soul from the memories.
When the lines of life and fate finally crossed,
there is still that second life, the one that lives on
even stronger in bonds than before.
We know that though they are gone
it is not the end, for their endeavors and their legacy.
As their life becomes a part of who we are,
like the new branching roots of a tree,
in the way we celebrate their past and live for what is coming.
To prove to ourselves that we are still strong. We are alive,
and it is finally our time to hit the ground—running.

Broken Things

We like broken things,
    the ones that remind us of ourselves,
because we see the pieces to be put back together
    but instead decide
        to let it stay broken.
Maybe it's because we see ourselves in
    the shards of glass
        carelessly strewn across the floor
    like the teenage lives we hold.
Disoriented and disorganized,
    there is no real answer;
        no real way to put the puzzle
    back together.
But maybe
    that's the point.
        Maybe it's supposed to be this way.
    Maybe we just break
        into p i e c e s,
and nobody wants to take the time
        to put us back
            together.

Want

Sometimes there can be a want for the unknown,
unknown because we have not been shown
exactly what we want;
we just know only... the want.

Who You Were

When I said I loved you, it was nothing but true.
You're not the same boy I fell in love with at first sight;
you're not the same boy who told me to jump into flight
just so you could catch me. You're just not the same.

I see you every day, but the only similarity is your name.
You used to be your own person, but now you follow the crowd.
You were quiet and fun; now you're obnoxious and loud.
What happened to the boy who would hold me while I cried?

Something happened. I don't know what; I don't know why
the tables have turned. Everything has
changed. I can't love you like this.
I miss who you used to be, the one deserving of my first kiss,
but that was then and this is now.
You're just not you.

Giving Up

Simply saying the words "I'm done,"
giving up on it all.
Trying and trying over again,
not having the energy to fall
and get back up again—
the loss of all willpower.
Like not being able to bring back
the life of a wilting flower—
tired and exhausted,
just simply going through
the motions of life.
While everything we do
means nothing to us.
None of it matters
to the rest of our lives,
to our future and what happens later.
All of it is pointless.
We ask why we are here.
Because after giving up
we have only ourselves to fear—
of what we might say
or what we might do,
knowing none of this will ever
bring me closer to you.

Free, Wild, and Young

Let's go somewhere, just get away.
Tell me that everything's going to be okay,
that we can just be together, you and me.
As we hold onto each other during a scary movie
and find excuses to be crazy and to not care
about anything else, no matter where
we are with nothing to lose—only to gain
our time of immortality, kissing in the rain.
It's who we are, free, wild, and young.
We are different, yes; we stand out among
everyone else because all that I know
is that I love you and you love me.
So let's get away, set ourselves free,
'cause together, there is nothing we can't be.

What Does It Mean

What does it mean to be?
Is it simply to embody ideas of life
and be?
Or is it something bigger—
to completely understand the truth?

What does it mean to live?
Can you simply breathe in and out
and live?
Or does it involve hurt, and loss, and beauty—
to live life completely?

And what does it mean to believe?
Does one simply understand everything heard
and believe?
Or does life test those limits, blur the lines—
to believe in the unseen?

But to be a believer in life...
The life of one who gets to be different,
gets to believe
in love, in freedom, and that one small chance—
to live, to believe, and to be
anything.

The Dark Sun

They say that we should let go of all the bad people in our lives, the people who invite the darkness. The ones who like to step on boundaries, the people who fight fire with ice on the boundaries we shouldn't be crossing. They told us to let go of those people, but what if that is not quite possible? What if I am that person ...

What if the bad seed in my life is me?

Because I always seem to be chasing happiness, but the closer I get, my mind decides to let it slip. And when it slips, I do too. All happiness goes out the window, and I wonder if I ever wanted happiness, if I wanted to feel okay or if I just wanted to fail yet again. Because the closer I seem to reaching the sun, the more I want to be in the dark.

No Second Chance

Do you know how easy it is to lose a life? Just reckon,
to be here one moment and gone the next, somehow
it only takes fourteen seconds.
Anything can happen in a random moment, an errand;
you cease to exist with one wrong turn, a missed step. Life allows
for it to be so easy to lose your life, still reckon.
When we are young, we are free; they beckon
to say there is so much we have at our fingertips, how
we have more than fourteen seconds, don't be frightened.
Or at least that's what they tell us, saying as it happened
that we are too invincible. We avow
it's not that easy to lose our lives, we reckon.
But what if it is? What if we have control
of every single millisecond?
What if we have the power to make it stop, to end it now?
Though they thought I had all the seconds
in this world I abandoned.
Because without hesitation, I had no more
reasons—only one set end.
No more holding myself back; the decision was easy anyhow.
Do you know how easy it was to take my life? I reckon,
it only took a second.

I Fell in Love

Just one quick blink and somehow
everything in the world came crashing down.
And darkness never felt so real, so blinding—
a quiet, cold feeling, spreading from heart to mind
like poison, making me think and believe
that everything found is meant to be lost again.
Like feeling that this life I have shouldn't belong to me
because I am not worth it.

But that was before you opened my eyes.

Through the darkness, your hand found my own,
pulling me into the light,
and once our eyes met I understood
that I could breathe and live,
but had never truly lived a day in my life.
Now, looking at you, I am awake to find
that faith itself shines brightly in your spirit.
You have brought back what I once lost:
a sense of connection.
So I blinked one more time and
I fell in Love.

Being Young

Do you remember what it's like to be young and to be free? Because that is where we all are now. This is our present, our reality—high school. This is our chance, the only shot we are going to get. Dream big, sing out loud, imagine what the future holds. Right now is where we need to be. To live and to breathe in this scent of freedom, catching in the air, riding on the dreams we know each one of us has.

So why don't we chase them? Do something stupid and find a way to figure out who we are and be willing to make dumb mistakes in the process and forgive ourselves. Because that is just who we are; we're young and damn proud of it. We're teenagers but not quite legal; we're part of the ultimate crossroads between growing up early or staying young for that little bit longer.

So hold on to it—the children we still are. Take risks, fall in love, break some hearts, follow our own ... This is the time to do it, to do all the things we say we can. Because we're young, we're free, we can breathe, and this is our reality.

Broken Girl

What do you do with a broken girl
who owns a life she does not deserve?
For she looks in the mirror every single day
to see the bruises and scratches from the past.
How can she be expected to move on from that
after being strong for so many years?
And how do you stop the tears from falling,
knowing you cannot change what she's been through?

But is there a way to give back that life she had
or replace the love that she has lost?
To put her heart seamlessly back together again
without forgetting any of her delicate pieces?
And how do you tell her that she's beautiful,
that life will be okay at the end of it all?
That it is all right to cry, to let it out,
to let her scream at the top of her voice
that this life she has isn't worth it?
She cannot feel anything at all anymore,
that she didn't mean to do it,
she doesn't deserve to be happy.

How do you convince that girl
that she deserves the whole world?
It is okay to ... to not be okay.
Shit happens, but life goes on, and someday—
someday she may look back at this and realize
she made it, that things do get better.
And for that she might grow a little stronger,
dry her tears,
and be okay again.

Outsider

He didn't really hear much of what they were saying; everything sounded so distant.

Watching their actions, laughing, and talking—he didn't feel like a part of it anymore.

Because he is surrounded by people—people who love him, people he loves,

and it doesn't mean anything to him, not right now, not in this moment.

As it all starts building, the anger, the confusion, and the depression each amplifying one another, battling inside of his chest until the breaking point.

His breaking point of too many emotions as the battle begins to win out,

slowly, piece by piece, he starts breaking until he falls apart completely.

It starts with the inside, everything building up so close to a boil until it all spills over, consequently leading to the next part,

where his hands start shaking. There is no longer a chance to go back.

Because that is when the tears start falling, quietly, but nonetheless everything comes pouring out, uncontrollable and completely uncensored,

without any adherence to the notions he kept about letting others in.

It's all gone, his ability to hold onto everything, to keep himself together.

The emotions finally take over, consuming every ounce of control he once had...

And maybe that is the worst part, the part that terrifies him the most: the idea that he has lost it, the control over everything he thought he was,

That he has no choice. He has no places left to hide.

Because now they are on the inside; he has let them all in and there is no going back.

Take a Moment

You know those days, those hours, those moments
where the world somehow seems to slow down a little bit
and it's almost as if time is finally on your side,
as if life is giving you a chance to breathe again.
So in that moment, you don't just spend it all at once—
no, you hold onto it, you understand it. You feel it.
The opportunity to finally stop and quiet down the thoughts
of whatever goes on in your life, all the little things.
It all just disappears, and in that moment, silence is beautiful.
Quiet enough to hear your heart beating with time you now hold.
Because maybe you made it, it's not all over, but just for a second
you feel better and you can forget the pain and the scars; you can
live again.

What's Next

You know how sometimes, there's something you really want, and you've wanted it for a really long time, but your mind just can't let it go. So you try and try again until you finally get it, until you have finally reached what you've dreamed about for so long? Once you get it, though, it's never the same, is it? Like things aren't what you expected; it's not as worth it or perfect as you thought it would be.

It's like maybe you fell in love—with the idea of something rather than what it really was. Because once it became real, so did your disappointment when you realized that the idea you had in your head was wrong all along. Then you're stuck on the same crossroads question everyone else runs into: What do you do now?

Blossoming Red

The touch of metal, its cold, sharp chill
runs through her veins right down to her skin.
As one by one, slowly, her fingers close hard on the straight line,
on the sharp point
as the small rose blooms—no subtle red tint,
the bright succulent red, a stain under the skin
growing brighter
by the second.

Unforgivable

He heard it hit the ground and he swore he heard his heart break
with it.
Because in that moment, it was all over. He had failed.
He had failed the moment the metal hit the ground and he missed it.
He couldn't believe he missed it.
He couldn't take it. He couldn't get the sound out of his head;
the bounce, the impact, the cold chill of his own mistake.
There was nothing he could do to make up for it later;
he had to walk away
before the tears began to fall, silently but so undeniable
and his body started shaking. He needed to get out,
out of his mind, out of the world, away from the mistake,
somewhere he could breathe.
Because in that moment, he let them down. He let everyone down,
including himself. He couldn't breathe; he was choking himself with
tears
of frustration, disappointment, shame, and a burning apology.
But he still can't forgive himself for it.
He doesn't think he ever will.

Missing Pieces

Houses and houses add up in one colorful blur,
and sometimes he wishes he could slow it all down.
He wonders what happens beyond those walls—
behind the front door, what are those people's lives like?
Are those people truly happy with the lives that they live?
He asks this every time the houses begin to blur
because he finds himself asking the mirror that same question,
and it's a damn shame when he realizes that the answer is no.
The sad part is, he doesn't even know how to fix himself,
but maybe it's just a part of growing up, being a teenager—
the screaming, the crying. He swears his hands will never stop
shaking
with the worry that this will not change, that it will not get better.
So he passes all those houses, the beautiful blurred lines of color,
and he wonders what the lives inside are really like.
Because he wants to know if they are happy, if they are all okay,
or if any of them are like him: broken and unable to find the right
pieces to be fixed.

A Kiss and a Slap

A kiss on the cheek, then a slap to the face.
Add an excuse and an apology
before he took another drink
and started all over again.
Because he seemed to enjoy it, this game
of her being the puppet
while he pulled the strings
attached to her heart
without a care or a shred of conscience
for her loss of dignity,
or for whom she could be beyond the scars.
For the bruises he left behind.
Someday it will end, by the hands of God
or by her own, because in the end
she will finish this, and soon enough
it will be over, before he can blink.
He will never
Ever
touch her again.

I Wish It Were Love

Some days I wish I were in love with you.
It would give me a reason to feel the way I do.
To miss you all the time, to see you every day,
to try to drink in your presence as if I can preserve it
and hold onto who you are, to have a piece of you with me.
Your smile or your laugh or even how you look at people,
because some days I think I'm in love with you,
even when I know I'm not.

Holding out for Love

So maybe you feel worthless, like you're never going to be good enough.

Maybe you feel like nobody ever needs you as much as you need them.

But someday, maybe not today, someone will come into your life and show you all the love that you hand out to others.

They will love you unconditionally and care about you more than you could ever know.

And on that day, you will feel like more than a million dollars; you will feel loved.

Because not only do you love someone, but they love you back just as much.

You can't ask for anything more beautiful or worth it than that.

You just have to wait and be strong.

You'll find them in time.

Love Happens

So maybe we don't choose the ones we love.
Maybe sometimes it just happens
and we decide to accept it.

Pretty People

It's a shame to see such pretty people so sad.
All the beauty in the world cannot fix these broken souls.
And as the time runs out and the days wear thin,
the night comes on back, leaving only darkness to hold,
the beauty of the light fading into the sadness of the soul.
As we walk, your hands in mine on this lonely dark road,
together we are here and our thoughts echo off the bare walls.
While I can feel that you are broken, I can hear it in your heart.
And it's a shame to see such pretty people fall apart.

All Is Lost

It was there; she could feel it silently spreading through her veins.
The small feeling of hope and even a desire to just love life.
Because lately she hasn't been living or talking or hoping.
Somewhere along the way, she lost it and couldn't find her
way back.
But a moment ago, she truly could feel its warmth within her body,
the hope of a bright future, one with beauty and the promise of
life.
So once again when she lost that hope, and in that moment
she felt herself slip,
she knew that she had lost it again; not just hope,
but herself.

Looking Back

It felt good to know that it was over,
    to not feel any of those memories,
        the shadows blurring her vision
           or the weight pulling on her heart.
It was nice to look around and truly see the smiles,
    the happy laughter echoed by the birds
        and to see the little things that she missed, like every color
           of a sunset— no longer black-and-white.
Looking back, she knew that it had gotten bad,
    out of control even; she was slowly just slipping.
        Losing the grasp of her own reality, of the
           immensity of what she needed to deal with.
But somehow, she found her feet again—
    got lost in music, and life, and herself.
        She found her way out and it is beautiful
           because she can finally breathe again.

A Lesson Learned

She's insecure in her own skin,
though most people don't really know *why*.
She worries about the scars on her body,
about how difficult they are to hide.
Because they define the mistakes of her past
and everything she thought herself to be:
a one-out-of-six, *a statistic,*
that most people can't understand, do not see.
She is scared, the lonely kind of isolated,
the way her mind replays and goes back to
the moment it happened, what she did to deserve it.
Though in the end no one does. If only she knew
how to protect herself, how to stay safe.
How to know what to be, what she needed to say.
Or in the aftermath, how to put herself back together again,
that soon enough, she would somehow be okay.
But she will be stronger next time. She hopes and she prays
that maybe she will be guarded and able to show
the man who stole her dignity, her faith, and her pride
how damn good she has gotten at saying no.

Love Hurts

I think I understand it now,
　　the cycle of pain in our lives.
　　　This rampant running darkness
　　　　that we will never overcome.
　　　　　When we're okay, everything feels all right
　　　　　and we are free.
　　　But when we love them and they are hurting,
　　it hurts to know that we cannot change it.
Because we love them too much to know
　　that there is nothing that we can do.
　　　When they are hurting because their loved ones are hurting,
　　　　and all that is left behind is love and pain.
　　　　　We then hurt for them as they hurt for others
　　　　and the cycle begins
　　　all over
　　again.

It Hurts to Learn

I feel like the world is hurting
and I can't change any of it.
All the sadness, the pain, and the suffering
running rampant through our lives.
Yet here we are, the survivors of it all,
living through another day of each,
asking ourselves to just keep going.
To be strong enough to see tomorrow.
But what happens when our strength begins to fail,
when we are no longer enough?
What do we do when we know that it hurts
and that we have no control?
We push through it; we simply endure,
hoping to make it through one day, one moment.
Because we may begin to understand
that pain itself is necessary
and that sometimes we only understand things
when they hurt.

I Wish

I wish I could tell you that I need you,
    that I am lonely and I am tired.
        That I need you by my side.
I wish I could show you that I want you,
    that I adore you and everything you are.
        That I want my arms around you.
I wish I could tell you that I love you,
    that I love every piece of you.
        That I would love to know your mind.
And I wish I could tell you that you complete me,
    that you might be everything I have been looking for.
        That you might be *it*.

Did You Notice?

After talking to someone for a while, did you notice the "I love you" suddenly change to "Love ya,"

or maybe the "okay" transposed to "k"?

Did you see when the "babe" and "baby" became nothing more than a period?

Did you ever notice that?

And when you did, did you notice that it hurt?

Did you realize that somehow you were about to lose them, that they were slipping away from you?

Were you able to connect the dots and understand that somewhere between the time it all began up until now, that things have changed—that you've changed?

Because I bet you noticed.

And I bet it hurt.

Then you knew that there was no way to get them back.

Because in that moment, their hand slipped away from yours and they were gone.

Out of Place

Does tired even compare to that feeling anymore,
  that hopeless, empty, insignificant feeling
that she's trapped in a place where she does not belong
  in her life surrounded by all the things she is not?
Her beautiful friends and their beautiful minds
  that she cannot compare to.
Her too-smart classes with her too-smart classmates
  whom she does not fit in with...
Somehow she's here, existing in between the lines
  where people do not look and do not care.
Do not see her here, past the beauty and the brains,
  back to where she is stripped down to nothing but a face.
That nobody remembers and nobody needs to,
  as she is just another person in this world.
One without the beauty and one without the brains,
  one that nobody seems to want to claim.
And that is okay too; she knows it will happen
  When she looks in the mirror and sees who she is.
Because in the end it's her life, something of her own making,
  and she is just simply out of place.

Trust in Love

Do you ever fall in love with someone's words,
>the way their lips describe the secrets of their soul?

As if their words are what make them who they really are,
>as if they somehow pull you closer than their arms ever could.

It's almost like what they have to say is something so private
>that when they finally let you in, that's when it all begins.

Because at that point they've let down their guard, no more walls,
>and there is nothing keeping you from hurting them.

But maybe that's the point, the reason words are the secret;
>maybe it's because they've finally let you in. There is nothing left.

And there is nothing stopping you from hurting them, no walls to
break through,
>while they are simply trusting you not to break their heart.

A Waking Nightmare

They leaked into her dreams last night:
    the emotions, the tears, the emptiness.
It was terrifying, going to sleep like that, and somehow
    it all came crashing into her mind while she slept.
And she was crying, not just crying, but gasping, sobbing—
    it wouldn't stop.
She couldn't breathe, but the tears just kept coming and
    she couldn't do anything about it.
The tears fell faster while each breath raked her body with force—
    she gasped for air.
She thought she wouldn't make it.
    She couldn't breathe, and her vision was blurred with pain.
It hurt so badly that night,
    until
she woke up
    and she felt nothing.
Her chest seemed empty.
Riddled with scattered thoughts of dreams and what they left behind,
    her mind was too full to comprehend any of it.
She just knew that it hurt,
    watching herself fade away like that.

Printed in the United States
By Bookmasters